What will they say?
30 FUNERALS IN 60 DAYS

Allison Clarke

PHOTO CREDITS:
Kirsti Holley Photography (except where noted), Jeff Snyder Photography (p. 7), Allison Clarke (ch. 7, p. 31), Scott Roberts (ch. 9, p. 43), Fain Photography (ch. 29, p. 157)

What Will They Say? 30 Funerals in 60 Days

Copyright © 2012 Allison Clarke. All rights reserved. No part of this book may be reproduced or retransmitted in any form or by any means without the written permission of the publisher.

Published by Wheatmark®
1760 E. River Road, Suite 145,
Tucson, Arizona 85718 U.S.A.
www.wheatmark.com

ISBN: 978-1-60494-661-1
LCCN: 2012945655

Dedicated to my daughters
Jenna and Jamie

We only live once—go have fun!
–Allison Clarke

Author's Note

This book is a unique approach to living life with more appreciation and celebration. It is designed to give you practical tools and ideas to implement in your life today. There is a lesson from each person's life and research to support each idea.

Each chapter starts with a person in Portland who I admire and respect. Their photo and quote reflects the chapter's message.

A portion of the profit from this book will be donated to the charities these thirty people had passions for. Some of them are the American Heart Association, Boy Scouts of America, Oregon Humane Society, American Cancer Society, and individual trust accounts for their children.

To protect the privacy of others, all names, locations, and some stories have been changed in this book.

Contents

Author's Note v
Preface ix

1. The Sports Fan 1
2. Prankster 7
3. Ellis Island 13
4. Ski Racer 19
5. The Daughter's Letter 23
6. The Debater 27
7. Beaches 31
8. Art with Heart 37
9. Sheet Music 43
10. Strawberry Shakes 49
    Lessons Learned 55

11	Cherry Spitting Contests	57
12	Like a Brother	61
13	Caramel Corn	67
14	Track Walker	73
15	Bagpipers	79
16	World Map	85
17	Candles and Incense	91
18	Steelhead	97
19	Family Man	103
20	Rocks	109
	Lessons Learned	115
21	Sail Away	117
22	What's Wonderful?	123
23	Fresh Raspberries and Ice Cream	129
24	Cheerleader	133
25	The Photograph	137
26	Smile	143
27	Zip-a-Dee-Doo-Dah	147
28	Animal Lover	151
29	Courage	157
30	Square Dancer	163
	Lessons Learned	171

Conclusion ... 173

References ... 175

Preface

I was on a plane flying to Atlanta on my way to check off five more states I had been to: Georgia, Alabama, Arkansas, Mississippi, and Tennessee. I was reading Eckhart Tolle's book *The Power of Now* (1997). On page 44 he writes, "Fear seems to have many causes. Fear of loss, fear of failure, fear of being hurt, and so on, but ultimately all fear is the ego's fear of death, of annihilation. To the ego, death is always around the corner. In this mind-identified state, fear of death affects every aspect of your life."

That page got me thinking and I read it over several times. Before I left on my trip I was telling one of my friends that I feel such an urgency to live. I have my "Live Once" list and plan when I am going to make the experiences happen. So many people I know say, "One day I will . . ." "Someday I will . . ." or "I hope that I . . ." Most of the time they don't make it happen.

For sixteen years, I conducted training for corporations to help make their employees' lives better and improve communication. After each session, the attendees told me they were inspired to change relationships, take more risks, and reach realistic and meaningful goals. I know people can change, if they want to.

Four years ago, a guy in one of my classes told us a story about sitting next to an eighty-year-old woman on the plane. She asked him if he had his one hundred things he wanted to do before he died written down. He told her no and, after hearing this, he inspired me to start my own list. I started to dream of places I had not seen, sporting events I could attend, physical challenges like running a marathon I could do, and concerts I would enjoy.

I took my own advice and jumped out of my comfort zone. I started Allison Clarke Consulting. I had been told by many in my industry that speakers and trainers must write a book. The idea came to me on the plane to Atlanta! Go to funerals and listen to what impact the deceased had on the living. Thirty funerals in sixty days—it would be unique and interesting and would provide evidence that I could use to coach others. This would provide tools for us on how we choose to live our lives. What I didn't expect is how much the thirty people would change the way I live my life.

My passion to live in the moment, travel, and appreciate people became confirmed and stronger.

In the thirty funerals I never heard anyone talk about how much they loved the person's car, house, or watch; it was all about the experiences and adventures they shared with the deceased. This life is not meant to be a selfish one; it is a place where we can teach, mentor, and mold others. Ask yourself this: how is someone's life better because they crossed your path in life?

Close your eyes and imagine that today is your last day. What are your best memories and what didn't you make happen? Perhaps a relationship was left damaged or neglected, a trip was never taken, or you never learned piano or jumped out of the airplane. It could be a simple as never teaching someone how to make your favorite pie. How did you help others? When people met you, did you leave a positive impression on them? Will people remember your smile or your temper?

When I arrived back in Portland from my trip to Atlanta, I started my

Preface

funeral project. My first action was meeting with a funeral home. I ran the idea by the general manager, Marie, and she loved it. She gave me a few links where I could read the obituaries. Every morning, I got online and read about strangers' lives. I picked the people based on what I read about them. The ages ranged from thirty-five to 104 and a half, and included fifteen men and fifteen women.

Why do we wait to see some of our friends and family only at weddings and funerals? Why don't we make time and plan events to see them? Why do we wait until people are sick or hurt sometimes to get in touch?

I attended the funeral of my friend's mom in 2008. My friend Joan talked about the impact her mother-in-law had had on her three kids and how much Joan appreciated her. After I left that service, I went home and wrote Shirley, my mother-in-law, a letter of thanks for making a difference in the lives of my daughters. She is at most events from school plays to sporting events. She takes them to the Enchanted Forest amusement park, bakes cookies, reads, plays dolls, and makes crafts with them. How many times do we wait and tell people how we feel when they no longer can hear us?

Now, I would go discover lessons from people I never had the opportunity to meet. I would only feel and hear about how they made an impact on others. I dressed in black, put on my pearls that my dad gave me at my wedding, and went to funeral number one.

"No one wants to die. Even people who want to go to heaven don't want to die to get there. And yet death is the destination we all share. No one has ever escaped it. And that is as it should be because Death is very likely the single best invention of Life. It is Life's change agent. It clears out the old to make way for the new. Right now the new is you, but someday not too long from now, you will gradually become the old and be cleared away. Sorry to be so dramatic, but it is quite true.

Your time is limited, so don't waste it living someone else's life. Don't be trapped by dogma—which is living with the results of other people's thinking. Don't let the noise of others' opinions drown out your own inner voice. And, most important, have the courage to follow your heart and intuition. They somehow already know what you truly want to become. Everything else is secondary."

Excerpt from Steve Jobs's 2005
Commencement Address
to Stanford University

What will they say?

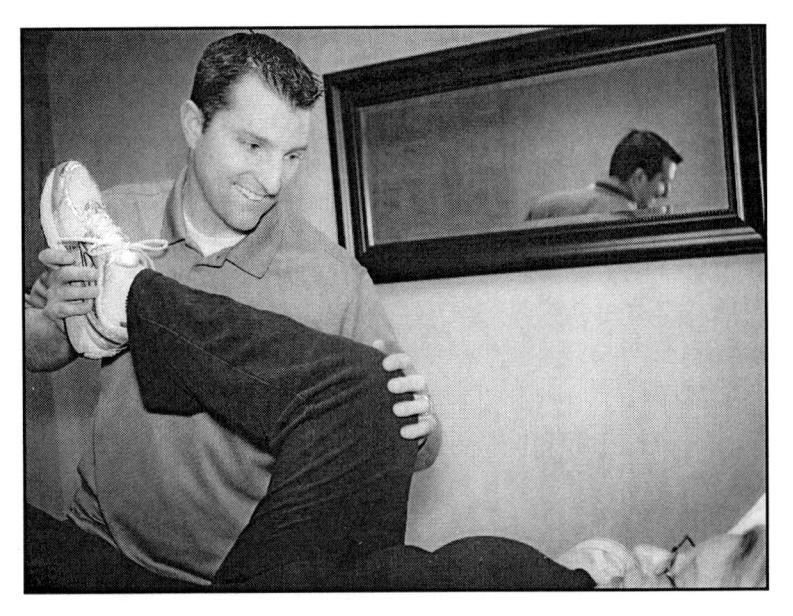

Dan Morlan *(co-owner with his wife, Melissa, of Active Edge Physical Therapy & Sports Medicine)*

Chapter 1

"The impetus was to be able to have more one-on-one time with our patients and to be a part of the community we live in. Melissa and I felt strongly that there will always be a place for a business that puts its clients before profit and the results have been wonderful. Success is really more a factor of what your measuring stick is . . . the typical measuring stick in business is profits, but we feel successful because we are making great connections with our community and loving what we do because we have time to really work with our patients on a very personal level. We take time to truly listen."

> "Listening is a magnetic and strange thing, a creative force. The friends who listen to us are the ones we move toward. When we are listened to, it creates us, makes us unfold and expand."
>
> KARL MENNINGER

The Sports Fan

Funeral number one was held for a woman, "Carol," who had lived to be seventy-nine years old. I picked her service because of her passion for basketball.

As I drove up to the church, I was wondering how this was going to work. Would people stop and ask me why I was there, how I knew her? I gave this lots of thought. When my grandmothers died, would I care if a stranger attended the funeral because they were intrigued by her life? No, I would want people to be there to hear the stories that we shared because she was an amazing person. Perhaps they would leave inspired to help animals, donate time to charity, and make people laugh.

This chapel was located in a retirement community. As I walked in, there were many residents chatting and laughing; I didn't feel sadness in the air. Some had walkers or canes and one woman had a purple cast on that had been signed by her friends. Average age was about eighty. As I watched these women connect, I saw myself in them. One day I will be like that.

I signed the guest book and took a program. My dad grew up in New York and told me to always walk like you know where you are going.

I sat in the back and observed the people. There were about 175 people there, and everyone smiled at me as they entered. Most people were dressed up, men in suits and women in dresses. I stared at the stained glass with wheat and grapes as I waited for the service to start.

We started to hear the stories about Carol. She had been on the winning team in the forties for her Catholic school's basketball team. I wondered how that was because women didn't play much then on private school sports teams. We were told about how, if they lost, the nuns would cry. It was a big piece of her life. She had passion for the NBA and was a Portland Trailblazer fan.

Carol had many different chapters in her life and left an impact on many. They said she took one day at a time and was a true friend. "Ave Maria" was sung by a woman in her late seventies; it gave me chills. What a wonderful voice and gift to give to others. Her son spoke about the difference she made in her granddaughters' lives. She was a true mentor as she lived with them for twenty years. She had a unique ability to listen when you had a problem and ask questions until you had found your own answer.

After the service was over, I walked out feeling inspired to be a better listener and to sing aloud more often. During the service I had sung along with the *Panis angelicus*, a song that I hadn't sung for twenty-five years. It reminded me of my years singing with the Colorado Children's Chorale. I walked out of the chapel, got into my car, and wrote a few notes: "A person with passion for people and sports." As I thought about the life of this fine woman, I realized she had been a good leader, not in a flashy way but in a quiet, unassuming way. I thought of several examples and relevant quotations.

In business we can lead people more effectively when we truly listen, just as Anne Mulcahy did.

An article by Gary Burnison in *Bloomberg Businessweek* states, "Anne Mulcahy, who recently retired as chairman of Xerox Corp. (XOX), recounted to me her experiences during the dramatic turnaround of that company, which in the early 2000s seemed headed toward bankruptcy. She met with employees personally not only to explain the company's plan, which included layoffs, but also to listen to their fears, concerns, ideas, and their desire to restore the company's profitability and reputation.

"As Mulcahy illustrated, leadership is much less about the leader, and much more about the followers and the mission. It's about having individuals look into your eyes and see who you, as the leader, really are; it's about letting them see into your soul. That kind of transparency and connection starts with listening.

"More than charisma, real leadership is about being authentic, which is a trait that endures. Leadership is also about compassion and the genuine development of the people you are leading. Leadership is never about the one who leads; it is always about the team and the organization. Leadership is about helping people feel sufficient common purpose so that they are able to achieve extraordinary things" (Burnison 2010).

John Quincy Adams, the sixth president of the US, said it best: "If your actions inspire others to dream more, learn more, do more, and become more, you are a leader."

"To listen well, is as powerful a means of influence as to talk well, and is as essential to all true conversation."
CHINESE PROVERB

Lesson #1
Listen and lead others to their own answers.

Kendra Matthews *(partner, Ransom Blackman LLP, sharing a light moment with nephew, Liam, and niece, Sophia)*

Chapter 2

"I have never been in a situation—personal or professional, joyful or tragic—in which a positive attitude wasn't an asset. While my attitude cannot always change the outcome, it can, almost always, change the experience. Why not make it a positive change?"

> "This is what it's all about. If you can't have fun at it, there's no sense hanging around."
>
> JOE MONTANA

Prankster

The second funeral I attended was held for an eighty-one-year-old man, "David." I selected this service because he looked like a friendly person in his picture.

This modest-looking church was very different from my first one. It was much more casual, both in the building and the attire of the people. I signed in, grabbed a program, and sat in the back. There were over one hundred people and I was sitting in the back on a bench with the babies. I didn't want people to talk to me, so I pretended to be reading the program. This would normally take me two minutes to read but, somehow, I read it for fifteen minutes. I was way out of my comfort zone. I always make eye contact and start conversations; it was killing me not to talk, and I didn't want to be asked why I was there. I learn so much about people by initiating conversations. I wanted the experience to be totally undercover so I could absorb human behavior at all levels.

Two words: energy and enthusiasm. The pastor did an amazing job creating an environment of fun. He pointed out that this was truly a celebration of David's life. He had us participating and clapping. The mic was open—my favorite style—and people began to telling their stories about how they were touched by David. We heard many funny stories about him playing pranks on his family, using baking powder in the gravy, and his fear of spiders. David's son told us that he heard a gunshot and ran upstairs; his dad was shooting at a spider—that is fear!

David's grandson sang a few songs and we watched a slideshow. I connected to David through his pictures. I began to like him. He had so many fun family photos featuring his big smile. I felt like I knew him when it was over. What pictures will people show about your life? After people see those pictures, will people connect and like you?

The stories people remember often include humor. With so much negativity around us, what are we doing to make others laugh and smile?

I left the service pumped up by the pastor's energy and facilitation. Later that day, I was dealing with something negative. I told myself that David would not let that get to him. He made me think differently and I moved on. It was odd that this stranger was on my mind and having an influence on me. How are we influencing others to think differently?

I choose to fly Southwest airlines because of their people. I am always entertained by the flight announcements and their associates. They are down-to-earth and connect with people well.

From the book *Nuts! Southwest Airlines' Crazy Recipe for Business and Personal Success* by Kevin Freiberg (1996, 67), you learn about Herb Kelleher's, the CEO of Southwest Airlines, approach to hiring. He insists on hiring employees with a good sense of humor. In filling any position Kelleher says, "We look for attitudes; people with a sense of humor who don't take themselves too seriously. We'll train you on whatever it is you have to do, but the one thing Southwest cannot change in people is inherent attitudes." In fact, during job interviews, job candidates are specifically asked to give an example of how they're recently used their sense of humor on the job and how they've "used humor to defuse a difficult situation."

This approach has helped make Southwest Airlines the most successful airline in the country. Employees love working for Southwest and do whatever it takes to sustain high levels of performance and quality service. And they have fun in the process!

How can you bring more fun and laughter into your job and life?

"The most wasted of all days is one without laughter."
E. E. CUMMINGS

"Laughter is an instant vacation."
MILTON BERLE

"The human race has only one really effective weapon and that is laughter. The moment it arises, all our harnesses yield, all our irritations and resentments slip away, and a sunny spirit takes their place."
MARK TWAIN

Lesson #2
Create an environment of energy, enthusiasm, and fun for people.

Regina Ellis *(founder/CEO Children's Cancer Association, a national organization inspired after her oldest daughter's death from cancer in 1995)*

Chapter 3

"Intense desire, passion, and courage create its own possibilities. With practice, I realized I could blow through barriers and accomplish goals I once imagined impossible."

"Vision without action is a daydream.
Action without vision is a nightmare."

JAPANESE PROVERB

Ellis Island

The third funeral I attended was held for a woman, "Hilda," who had immigrated to the United States from Austria in the 1920s and had reached the astounding age of 104 and a half. She must have had many adventures.

Hilda's service was held at a small funeral home rather than a church. As I sat in my car in the parking lot waiting for the time to go in, I noticed there were only about eight cars there. It would be a bit more challenging to blend in with the group. Feeling a bit uncomfortable, I entered the funeral home. I walked over and looked at her pictures and articles about her, including her documents from Ellis Island.

The family was on one side where we couldn't see them and that left the ten of us non-family members to sit in the main section. I sat in the third row from the back. As I waited for the service to start, they had "Ave Maria" playing and there was a strong odor of perfume. I stared at Hilda's white coffin and thought of her life. I pictured her going to all her friends' funerals and being the last one to go. Two women in their sixties, dressed in black from head to toe, looked back at me; I am sure they were wondering who I was.

The priest approached the lectern and explained that he had only known Hilda for about five months. He talked about how impressed he was with her ability to stay positive, be gracious, and appreciate others. Imagine that you are 104 and a half; what a challenge it would be to stay positive. He told us that Hilda had grown up in Austria during World War I. When her husband became ill, she became a certified nursing assistant. Helping others was a passion of hers. She had many grandchildren and great-grandchildren that she influenced.

He said Hilda retired when she was eighty-five. She couldn't take it and went back to work until she was ninety-six! That made me think about all stories we hear about people dying after they retire because they lose purpose and don't set a new vision of life. At 104 and a half, she taught us to stay busy and make a difference. I thought of one of my own experiences that related to the power of vision.

I recently stayed at the Four Seasons in Scottsdale, Arizona, to experience what Isadore Sharp—the founder, chairman, and CEO of Four Seasons Hotels and Resorts—had created. The valet was so engaging that I asked him what kind of training they provided for valets. He told me that they are trained to ask about twenty questions before they drop the luggage and leave the room! He knew more about me than the person who sat by me on the airplane for two hours because he was trained to engage and ask the right questions.

I bought Isadore Sharp's book in the gift store while I was there, *Four Seasons: The Story of a Business Philosophy* (2010). Here are a few parts that stood out to me:

How did a child of immigrants, starting out with no background in the hotel business, create the world's most admired and successful hotel chain? And how has Four Seasons grown dramatically over nearly half a century without losing its focus on exceptional quality and unparalleled service?

"The books may show that employees represent the largest share of expense. They don't show they can also earn the largest share of revenue. Or that long-term service employees are storehouses of customer knowledge, role models for new hires, and advisers for system improvement—all in all, our best source of added value. If employees are really doing their job, they're not a cost, they're an asset, our primary asset" (100).

"Our greatest asset, and the key to our success, is our people. We believe that each of us needs a sense of dignity, pride, and satisfaction in what we do. Because satisfying our guests depends on the united efforts of many, we are most effective when we work together cooperatively, respecting each other's contributions and importance." (Afterword)

"Life isn't about finding yourself. Life is about creating yourself."
AUTHOR UNKNOWN

> **Lesson #3**
> Have a vision for your life.

Eldridge Broussard *(motivational speaker and founder of Broussard Foundation Inc., a nonprofit 501c3 working with youth who overcame family deaths, the foster care system, and state prison)*

Chapter 4

"You are now becoming who you are going to become."

"It is literally true that you can succeed best and quickest by helping others to succeed."

Napoleon Hill

Ski Racer

The next funeral I attended was for "Andrew," a family man who had lived seventy-one years. I sat with two hundred other people in a large Episcopal church and heard people tell how this man had created some of the best memories in their lives. His eulogy said that he served the community with enthusiasm, integrity, and dedication. As I looked around I could see the impact Andrew had had on others.

Ski racing for his high school and college, Andrew took that talent and taught others his passion for the outdoors and skiing. He was involved with all of his six children from Boy Scouts to serving on the school board. He volunteered for over thirteen years with the Salvation Army.

He had so many interests that kept him interesting, active, and living a full life. His program read, "Andrew filled days of retirement with skiing, reading, gardening, photography, travel, cooking, fishing, hunting, camping, biking, and community service."

Music at this funeral made an impact. They had a piano, trumpet, violin, viola, and an amazing tenor. Andrew's granddaughters closed the ceremony with singing. You could tell the impact he had on his family as they shared their stories. I came away from this funeral encouraged and eager to share my talents with others.

The importance of mentoring came to mind. I discovered a memorable quote from Oprah Winfrey: "A mentor is someone who allows you to see the hope inside yourself" (http://www.quotesdaddy.com/quote/954969/oprah-winfrey/a-mentor-is-someone-who-allows-you-to-see-the-hope).

And I also found a website (http://www.hsph.harvard.edu/chc/wmy2008/wmy/intro.html) that tells us how notable people succeeded in part because of their mentors. Following is a quote from that site:

> Growing up, were there people in your life who encouraged you, showed you the ropes, and helped you become the person you are today? Think about family members, a teacher or coach, a neighbor, a boss, or family friend; those people were mentors to you.

Most successful people say they had mentors along the way who guided and encouraged them . . . Maya Angelou cites a grade school teacher who sparked her love of poetry; Quincy Jones points to the powerful influence of musician Ray Charles; and Sting credits a teacher whose energy inspired a lifelong passion for learning. Other participants include President Bill Clinton, Clint Eastwood, Cal Ripken, Jr., and Tom Brokaw.

How are you listening and guiding others?

Lesson #4
Share your talents by being a mentor.

Cynthia Malen *(respected leader at Fred Meyer, mother, wife, and grandmother)*

Chapter 5

"By appreciating others they feel valued and inspired. People become confident and they walk a little taller, with their heads a little higher. People are energized when they feel important and appreciated. You get to watch others 'light up'!"

> "There is more hunger for love and appreciation in this world than for bread."
>
> MOTHER THERESA

The Daughter's Letter

The fifth funeral I attended was for a man, "Danny," who had lived ninety-two years. His funeral was held at the small chapel within the nursing home where he had lived. As I walked into the chapel, I got a feeling for Danny before I read or heard anything. As we entered, there was a table with some of his belongings there. There was a teddy bear, golf club, and other golf items. What will represent your life? What is your most treasured possession?

I heard how Danny was an avid golfer and a mentor to many. His grandsons spoke on the influence he had on them. He taught them manners, golf, and the importance of respecting women and to care about their appearance.

Danny was truly committed to his family. His son-in-law stated that he felt Danny was a true father to him. Danny had written a letter to his daughter about how much he adored her and how proud she made him. He wrote and communicated his love for her often. As the letter was read, it made me cry. I was happy for their relationship and wishing that my girls and I had experienced that.

Danny's caregiver had written a letter to be read at the service. She talked about how polite and appreciative he was to her. He kept his sense of humor until the day he died.

How often do you find people complaining all the time? Here is a ninety-two-year-old man who remained positive because he made that choice.

So often we don't tell others how we feel and tell them only when it is too late. Why not show appreciation to others every day? It is the one thing people hunger for and crave more than anything. Most people leave companies because of lack of appreciation; it is rarely for a financial reason.

We remember how people make us feel. I was staying at the Boulders Resort in Arizona and the bellman was carrying my bags in for me. I had my laptop and several books in a bag. As he brought everything in, the straps on my bag ripped off, which was 100 percent my fault; I had put too much weight in the bag. He apologized over and over again, feeling bad. I told him not worry; it was not a big deal at all. My sister and I went to dinner at a local Mexican restaurant. When we returned to our room, there was a handwritten note from the man saying he was sorry about my bag and a wonderful tote bag with the Boulder's logo on it. Wow! That is true customer service! I have told that story to many and will return to the resort because of the way the staff made me feel.

> "The deepest craving in human nature is the craving to be appreciated."
> WILLIAM JAMES

> "Appreciation is a wonderful thing; it makes what is excellent in others belong to us as well."
> VOLTAIRE

Lesson #5
Show your appreciation to someone every day.

Ann Lam *(Immigrated to the United States from Vietnam in 1993 at the age of sixteen. In 2001 she opened her first nail salon and now owns three successful nail salons in the Portland area.)*

Chapter 6

"I challenge people to ask how they can do something, not if they can do something. Anything is possible."

> "Don't be afraid to challenge the pros,
> even in their own backyard."
>
> — COLIN POWELL

The Debater

The next funeral I attended was for a woman, "Liz," who was only sixty-one when she died. Her service was held at the large funeral home downtown. This service was crowded and promised to be a celebration of life rather than a sad event. When I walked in they were adding additional chairs in the back where I sat. We had extra time to wait for the celebration to begin. The funeral director had forgotten to order the limo, and the family had to make last-minute alternative travel arrangements. As I sat there, I pretended to read the program for fifteen minutes. At every funeral I found it fascinating that no one talked to me when I made myself look really busy.

This was one of the most colorful and high-energy services I went to. People were laughing and telling stories about Liz as we waited. I could feel the influence she had on them. When it was time for the mic to be open, there was a constant flow of people. Liz had had a huge influence on many Portland women. She taught them how to be dignified and the importance of education. She herself was always up on current affairs and ready to debate with many facts as evidence. She was known to challenge others by asking many questions.

Over ten people spoke, including neighbors, church members, friends, and family. Liz had influenced many in her different chapters of life. They encouraged others to keep her stories alive by telling them and to send e-mails and cards to the family to remind them what a difference she had made in their in lives.

A great example of someone who does this well is Oprah Winfrey. Back in 2006 she did her Pay It Forward Challenge. She gave over three hundred people in her audience one thousand dollars each and challenged them to come up with inspiring and creative ways to help others. Some of the chosen recipients included an orphanage, single and battered moms, homeless shelters, cancer research, inner city kids, fire victims, a pet-rescue organization, etc. Then in 2007, Oprah invited viewers to join in using their lives to improve the lives of others. What began as a campaign to encourage viewers to collect spare change evolved into the charity known as Oprah's Angel Network. More information on Oprah's Pay It Forward Challenge can be found at http://www.oprah.com/spirit/Pay-It-Forward-Stories.

What have you done to challenge others to make a difference?

"Do the things you think you cannot do."
ELEANOR ROOSEVELT

Lesson #6
Find a way to influence others for the better.

Allison Clarke *(On a trip to San Francisco, went sailing with Anthony Sandberg, owner of OCSC Sailing. Left to right: Melissa Maag, Lysa Johnson, Allison Clarke, Megan Garcia, Kendra Matthews, and Lori Wakefield.)*

Chapter 7

"Friends are my rocks in life. They keep me grounded, laughing, and changing. Traveling with people shows you who they really are."

> "A journey is best measured in
> friends, rather than miles."
> — Tim Cahill

Beaches

The next funeral was held at one of the major funeral homes in Portland for a sixty-nine-year-old woman by the name of "Anne." For the eulogy, a good friend read from Anne's journal. She had written about how much fun she had with her friends on their beach trips, the laughter, and connection they shared. They said that once she was your friend, you had a friend for life. She had written a part about her funeral, wondering who would attend and what they would say.

They talked about Anne's generous spirit and her sense of humor. They described her as having a "laugh-so-hard-your-belly-hurts laugh." She was confident and not intimidated by life. She had made a difference with her stepsons during her thirty years of marriage to their dad. She taught them how to live and love better.

Anne had a sense of adventure and traveled all over. She enjoyed camping, fishing, and cooking. She handled life with grace, dignity, and laughter.

Interestingly, Anne's stepsons had made her wooden coffin. It was beautiful and a reflection of their appreciation for her. They described her as "powerfully positive and strong in all she did."

As we sang the ballad "The Rose," I reflected on the words; we need to take chances, dance, and truly live. The music and lyrics were written by Amanda McBroom.

Some say love, it is a river
That drowns the tender reed
Some say love, it is a razor
That leaves your soul to bleed
Some say love, it is a hunger
An endless aching need
I say love, it is a flower
And you, it's only seed

It's the heart afraid of breaking
That never learns to dance
It's the dream afraid of waking
That never takes the chance
It's the one who won't be taken
Who cannot seem to give
And the soul afraid of dying
That never learns to live

When the night has been too lonely
And the road has been too long
And you think that love is only
For the lucky and the strong
Just remember in the winter
Far beneath the bitter snow
Lies the seed
That with the sun's love
In the spring
Becomes the rose

Here is an example I find fascinating about a company encouraging their employees to travel. It's from http://www.ucg.com/DisplayPage.aspx#980. "It concerns the company called UCG, one of America's leading, privately held providers of specialized business-to-business information. UCG employs approximately seven hundred employees and was recently voted one of D.C.'s Fifty Best Places to Work by *Washingtonian Magazine*."

UCG today officially disclosed to the media the spectacular details of its thirtieth Anniversary Company Trip to "Somewhere." Details of the trip, by far the most elaborate and complicated of any of the previous six trips that UCG has orchestrated to celebrate its amazing growth, had been kept secret for the two years it took to plan the surprise adventure.

A total of 1,030 UCG employees and guests made the all-expenses-paid trip to San Francisco, but were not told of their destination until they were on the plane, just hours away from landing. They spent the full Labor Day weekend treated to world-class celebrity entertainment, exclusive tours of the city, fine dining, and a magical excursion to Napa Valley wine country.

"The Trip to Somewhere, which we take every five years, is our special way of celebrating our success and thanking our employees and their significant others for their contribution to building a great company," said UCG cofounder Bruce Levenson.

Write your top five trips you would like to go on and when you will make them happen.

1.

2.

3.

4.

5.

"One's destination is never a place,
but a new way of seeing things."
HENRY MILLER

> **Lesson #7**
> Travel with your friends at every opportunity.

Jen DeBoer Roark *(friend, mother, dietitian, and wife)*

Chapter 8

"There will always be a daily 'To Do' list. It's inevitable. However, when opportunities arise to meet up with friends, I remind myself, 'People first, things second' and do my best to make that face time happen. The list can usually wait, the quality time and laughter with friends can't."

> "Your time is limited, so don't waste it living someone else's life."
>
> STEVE JOBS

Art with Heart

In Walter Isaacon's biography of Steve Jobs, Jobs talks about his passion for face-to-face communication. "There is a temptation in our networked age to think that ideas can be developed by e-mail and iChat," he said. "That's crazy. Creativity comes from spontaneous meetings, from random discussions. You run into someone, you ask what they are doing, you say 'Wow,' and soon you're cooking up all sorts of ideas." He then had the Pixar building designed to promote encounters and unplanned collaborations. "If a building doesn't encourage that, you'll lose a lot of innovation and the magic that is sparked by serendipity," he said, "so we designed the building to make people get out of their offices and mingle in the central atrium with people they might not otherwise see" (2011, 431).

This next celebration taught me the power of never letting your vision and passion die. The service was held for an eighty-year-old gentleman, "Paul," at a small country church. Paul had lived a long, productive life. He had worked in timber, finance, and the leasing industry. His true passion was art. Towards the end of his life, Paul had established his own art gallery and watched it bloom. His last three months were his most successful in business. How wonderful that he got to enjoy what he had created. How many people do we know who never take risks to do what makes them happy? I wish . . . One day . . . I always wanted to. . . . Paul made it happen!

Paul also had the opportunity to live with his sister and her children. He had made the commitment not to just be a signature on a card or voice on the phone. Through her tears, Paul's sister spoke up to say they enjoyed the power of the face-to-face interaction, something that so many people lack now in business and life.

Paul was a busy person who volunteered in the community, cooked gourmet food, and loved to run! He could be heard singing as he ran by neighbors. His positive attitude, sense of humor, and quiet determination inspired many.

Effective communication produces great success. The following is an excerpt from a CNBC.com interview with Duke basketball coach Mike Krzyzewski on October 20, 2010 (http://www.cnbc.com/id/39758819).

The head coach of Duke University's championship men's basketball team told CNBC Wednesday that frequent face-to-face communication is the way to develop a winning team, whether in sports or in business.

> "How do you make five guys on the court play like one?" said Coach Mike Krzyzewski, who has lead the Duke Blue Devils to four NCAA titles and coached Team USA to a gold medal in the Olympics. "How do you get a group of business people to play as one? You do that with constant communication. Face-to-face is the best way to communicate, where people can look each other in the eye and, when you have that opportunity, always to tell each other the truth and, [as a result,] an element of trust is developed."

Intel is a client of mine and I remember hearing about the No-E-mail Fridays. It is a way to get the employees to talk face-to-face to each other. As you walk around their cubicles, you see some people who sit a few cubicles away and choose to e-mail rather than walk a few feet to communicate.

We need to remember the 7-38-55 rule. According to a study Dr.

Albert Mehrabian conducted at the University of California in 1967, he found that words account for 7 percent, tone of voice accounts for 38 percent, and body language accounts for 55 percent of the message. They are often abbreviated as the "3 Vs" for Verbal, Vocal, and Visual. We need make sure the three parts of the message are congruent (Laneri 2009).

Be different and make time for face-to-face communication. Let's put down our devices and start conversations.

> **Lesson #8**
> Remember the value of face-to-face communication.

Aaron Meyer (concert rock violinist)

Chapter 9

"Music, to me is the world's only universal language. You can communicate with people in any part of the world through music even if you cannot speak the same language. Music touches our heart and soul and can deliver an amazing emotional message. I try to deliver this "amazing emotional message" when I perform by taking my listeners on a musical journey."

> "Music can change the world because
> it can change people."
> BONO

Sheet Music

The next funeral I attended was for a woman, "Kathleen," who had lived ninety-three years. This funeral was held at a small Catholic church nestled in a bustling neighborhood. There were about sixty people there and they joked that everyone in the neighborhood where she had lived for over sixty years was in attendance. The power of childhood friendships was stressed. So many chapters together with many ups and downs. There was a friendly and warm feeling in the room.

Kathleen had kept her mind sharp by doing crosswords and being an avid reader. She was in many book clubs and had joined her last one at the age of eighty-seven.

Kathleen's daughter gave one of the eulogies and I could see parts of her mother in her. Kathleen was very positive with a wonderful sense of humor. As parents, relatives, friends, or teachers, do we realize how much we are influencing our children?

They showed a picture of Kathleen in her late eighties wearing a Santa hat and being funny. When do we decide that we are too old to have fun? She had seen so much change: watching cable cars disappear and be replaced by automobiles and then having the cable cars be brought back to Portland.

Music was another passion of Kathleen's. There was sheet music all over the house and she was always playing the piano. The daughter remembered friends being over lots and there being fun energy around music. At the celebration, two of Kathleen's grandchildren played several of her favorite songs.

She raised three children by herself, and it was no surprise to read that she determinedly remained independent until she died. She was excited that, after renewing it, her driving license was valid until her one hundredth birthday! Knowing she loved the Oregon coast, her family released her ashes there.

We have all heard the theories and research on music's healing powers, but many believe that music can improve productivity as well. This is called the Mozart effect. I found a quotation on Kutchka.com (http://www.kutchka.com/products/musicincreasesproductivity.htm) that you may find interesting.

> We know that music can alter your mood. Films have been using musical scores for years to create the right mood for a scene. At times you hardly notice the music at all but you are very receptive to the mood being conveyed. So can we use music to put us in a "productive" mood?
>
> Research seems to support such a claim. For example, a trial where 75 out of 256 workers at a large retail company were issued with personal stereos to wear at work for four weeks showed a 10% increase in productivity for the headphone wearers. Other similar research conducted by researchers at the University of Illinois found a 6.3% increase when compared with the no music control group.
>
> What type of music is best? If your goal is to increase your concentration then music which has a constant, easy beat and light melodies are recommended. These are said to be good for those trying to study as they help you pace your reading to aid focus and memorizing. Baroque music is reported as an excellent example, especially the works of Vivaldi, Bach and Handel. Rock music can have a similar effect. According to a report in the journal *Neuroscience of Behavior and*

Physiology, the Russian Academy of Sciences discovered that a person's ability to recognize visual images, including letters and numbers, is faster when either rock or classical music is playing in the background. If you are aiming to be more productive through being more relaxed, then you may be interested to learn that research has shown that music with an upbeat rhythm can reduce stress hormone levels by as much as 41%.

What kind of music is in your workplace and how can you make an impact with it?

"Music is a moral law. It gives soul to the universe, wings to the mind, flight to the imagination, and charm and gaiety to life and to everything."
PLATO

Lesson #9
Fill your world with life-affirming music.

Cristi Jaksic *(friend and mentor to many)*

Chapter 10

"To have a friend, you've got to be a friend."

> "Do not go where the path may lead.
> Go instead where there is no path
> and leave a trail."
>
> RALPH WALDO EMERSON

Strawberry Shakes

The next funeral I attended was held for "Derek," a man who had lived to be nearly one hundred. He had met his wife at work and they were married for seventy years! The obituary didn't tell much about him, just his family that was left. The service was held in the side chapel at a funeral home far outside Portland. As usual, I entered the chapel and sat in the back. It seemed as though mostly family members were there; as I listened to Derek's son give the eulogy, I saw that family was everything.

This year on Father's Day, Derek's son "Nathan" made it a point to write a card and to get his father's favorite treat. Derek loved strawberry shakes from Jack in the Box! He swore it was better than any other chain. When Nathan delivered the shake, Derek asked him to read the card to him. Derek appreciated his son's thoughtful and unique gesture. His other son called him that day from the East Coast and Derek died the next day. Nathan expressed that giving the eulogy was the hardest thing he had ever had to do. I admired his courage for being up there. After Nathan finished, he went over and hugged his mother in her wheelchair. Derek had taught Nathan to love and respect people; he was a reflection of his father.

The fifty people who were there were reminded by the minister to invite the family to dinner or brunch and to send cards to let them know they have support. The assisted living facility where Derek had lived in recent years had sent along a note saying how wonderful it was to have him as a guest.

How can we do small, unique things for others to make a difference? From a milkshake to a card or even planning a surprise trip, there are many ways we can make difference.

Here is a good example of a person doing something special for another person (Robison 2008). It's the account of one hotel guest, Joanne Hanna, receiving special attention at just the right time.

> "The gentleman who escorted me to my room at the Ritz-Carlton asked how my day was, and I told him, the poor guy," says Hanna. "He said he'd be happy to book me into the spa, or send up a masseuse, or even have a rose-petal bath drawn for me, and I'd have loved all of that. But there was no time." So he told Hanna to wait a moment, and then he returned with a scented candle. "I was so touched, I was speechless—it was so thoughtful and helpful, like something a friend would do," says Hanna. "So I told the people at the desk. And now whenever I check into a Ritz-Carlton, there's a candle waiting for me."
>
> Perhaps any hotel employee could figure out that a tired and frazzled guest could use a little help. And maybe any hotel company with a global database could keep track of a candle-loving customer. But making sure that every employee notices, cares, thinks, and acts as thoughtfully as the one who served Hanna—well, that takes something special. The Ritz-Carlton calls that something special "The Ritz-Carlton Mystique."

Employees will only treat the customer as well as the employee is being treated. What are you doing that is unique to make people feel important?

"Unless you walk out into the unknown, the odds of making a difference in your life are pretty low."
Tom Peters

Lesson #10
Do something special and unique for someone.

Lessons We've Learned

1 Listen and lead others to their own answers.

2 Create an environment of energy, enthusiasm, and fun for people.

3 Have a vision for your life.

4 Share your talents by being a mentor.

5 Show your appreciation to someone every day.

6 Find a way to influence others for the better.

7 Travel with your friends at every opportunity.

8 Remember the value of face-to-face communication.

9 Fill your world with life-affirming music.

10 Do something special and unique for someone.

Hallie Janssen *(director of e-commerce marketing for Columbia Sportswear, wife, mother, and avid runner)*

Chapter 11

"There are too many things to enjoy in life and the key is finding the balance that lets you enjoy it all!"

> "Life is like riding a bicycle.
> To keep your balance you must keep moving."
> ALBERT EINSTEIN

Cherry Spitting Contests

The next funeral was held at a fairly large Church of Christ in Portland. The energy was contagious as I walked into this service. The funeral was being held for a man, "John," who had died at the age of fifty-nine. John's grandson, who was about thirteen, greeted the guests with confidence as we sat. There was a mixture of around one hundred people in the church sanctuary. John's story was told by his friends and family.

He had a met a single mom with three children and took on the responsibility of making sure they were taken care of. John gave his life to them, and, in the end, the loyalty was returned.

The friends and family described John's passion for politics, his neighborhood, and his community. He would speak up and give his time to make changes.

Out of one hundred people, six told stories about John. His daughter's eighth grade teacher came and talked about his dedication to his daughter's education, programs, and sports. He never missed a conference, game, or any event she was involved in. Fifteen years had passed and the teacher still remembered his impact.

Several neighbors spoke about the humor John brought to the neighborhood with his yard competitions and pranks he played. He had mentored and watched over the children in the neighborhood.

Coworkers told stories about John and the voice he brought to the company. They laughed as they remembered him. A representative from his union was there sharing examples of their interactions. The grandson who had greeted us at the door went up to speak. Without saying a word, I could see the influence John had had on him. This boy spoke from his heart and expressed his love for his grandfather, talking about their cherry spitting contests and other quality time John had spent with him.

The minister ended by talking about the loyalty between John and his wife. At the end of his life, she would pay back the loyalty, just as he had taken care of her and her children years ago when she was in need. The minister described John's life as a painting. Every person and experience added another brush stroke.

When we are gone, what will our painting look like? When others see it, how will we inspire and encourage them to keep adding strokes to their life? John lived an intentional life, making impacts on many areas of his life. He led a balanced life and connected with many.

"I'm serious when I do my work.
I'm not serious when I'm home with my kids."
BILL GATES

"If you're interested in 'balancing' work and pleasure, stop trying to balance them. Instead make your work more pleasurable."
DONALD TRUMP

Lesson #11
Connect with many people through a balanced life.

Colin Wall *(building engineer/after school art teacher at an Oregon primary school since 1995)*

Chapter 12

"When I remember those individuals who had the biggest impact on me, it was usually the ones who acted out of compassion, authenticity, and a sense of humor that I remember the most. I think it's important to carry that torch, undiminished, as you're not only honoring those before you but also expressing hope for the future."

> "You don't have to be a 'person of influence' to be influential. In fact, the most influential people in my life are probably not even aware of the things they've taught me."
>
> SCOTT ADAMS

Like a Brother

As I told more people about my book, they began to think of me when they heard about a life celebration. I received a text from a friend saying that his friend "Hassan" had committed suicide and the service was on Sunday.

As I approached the grand funeral home, I noticed a sea of mourners in black suits and formal black dresses entering the lobby. This was by far the most crowded funeral I had been to! I went in the side door, signed the guest book, and sat in the back row. There were two hundred chairs set out and all of them were filling up. When the service started, there were one hundred people standing in the back. Hassan's picture was up on the screen for all of us to stare at. Some relatives served us tea and pastries as we waited. The lobby was stocked with fruit platters, desserts, coffee, and punch.

I felt the loss of life at this celebration more than I had at the other services. His loved ones had not seen it coming and didn't have time to prepare or say `goodbye. As the service stated, the family said they wanted this to be a celebration of Hassan's life. The slideshow started off with pictures from his early life, before Hassan came to the US. As the slides become more recent, I stared at them, wondering what could have pushed Hassan to a place where he thought death would be better than living.

The slides showed that family was Hassan's true passion. You could see it in the photos. They showed pictures of his daughter's arms around his neck. Why did Hassan leave all these people who cared for him so much?

Eulogies were given by six of Hassan's male friends. The stories had the same theme. They loved him like a brother; they would have done anything for him and they are dedicated to taking care of his family now that he is gone. There was not a dry eye.

They described Hassan as a risk taker and a generous, hardworking man. He had helped many of his friends with any problem they had had. Did the pressure of work outweigh the other areas of his life? He had influenced so many; I wish he had been able to see his own life celebration.

As the casket was loaded into the hearse, there was more emotion. It was not fair to the living. We have to remind ourselves how many people we influence and that we have their support.

I left the funeral sadder but more appreciative of how my actions impact others. One day as I was working on my book, my ten-year-old daughter, Jamie, sat down and wrote this:

> My mom's motto is, "You only live once." That inspires me every day to live my life happily. She makes a list of what she wants to do before she dies—run a marathon, jump out of an airplane—and she did! She jumped out of an airplane and ran a marathon.

People

I see people walking down the sidewalk,
Most of them aren't smiling,
Sometimes I smile at them,
To try to make not only myself happy.
Others usually smile back and others don't.

My mom always smiles; she inspired me to write this.

I love you, Mom. −Jamie

What type of influence do you have on others and how can you make a bigger impact?

> "Think twice before you speak, because your words and influence will plant the seed of either success or failure in the mind of another."
> NAPOLEON HILL

Lesson #12
Remember that you are loved and make a difference to many people.

Shirley Ittershagen *(grandmother to my daughters, Jenna and Jamie)*

Chapter 13

"A true meaning of happiness is giving. It's not the recipes we pass on to others as much as it is the joy of giving, loving, and making memories."

> "No one who cooks, cooks alone. Even at her most solitary, a cook in the kitchen is surrounded by generations of cooks past, the advice and menus of cooks present, the wisdom of cookbook writers."
>
> — LAURIE COLWIN

Caramel Corn

The next funeral I attended was held for a woman by the name of "Sara," age forty-two. The service was small and held at a wood-framed church away from the city. The obituary stressed that the service was to be a celebration. And it was! As the mic was made available for Sara's life stories, a clear picture was painted of her. Loved ones described her as a very strong woman who would do "man's" work. It was challenging for her to express her feelings and to say she loved people. Sara was determined to fight her cancer as long as she could. She died as strong as she lived.

Her daughter spoke about Sara's caramel corn recipe. She loved making it and thinking of her mother. Sara's sister talked about fun adventures together, one being an all-day event at Kmart. They stayed there all day and hit every blue light special. Sara's cats made her happy and were a big part of her life that added comfort until the end. Cooking, animals, and outings with friends and family made this woman's life full.

Sara left this poem for the living, encouraging them to be strong and to live now!

> When I come to the end of the day
> And the sun has set for me
> I want no rites in a gloom-filled room.

Why cry for a soul set free?
Miss me a little, but not too long
And not with your head bowed low.
Remember the love we once shared—
Miss me, but let me go.
For this journey we all must take
And each must go alone.
A step on the road to home.
When you are lonely and sick at heart
Go to the friends we know
And bury your sorrows in doing good deeds—
Miss me, but let me go.

Teach others your recipes so they may bring happiness to others when you are gone. My grandmother in Long Island, New York, made her famous lemon tarts and passed the recipe down to my mother when she moved away to Colorado. My daughter Jenna, who is twelve, now bakes them at Christmas with me. Every time we make them, the smell brings me back to my holidays in Colorado. I want to share this recipe with you.

Sefton (Browne) Lemon Tarts

Makes 12 tarts

Heat oven to 400 degrees.

Make the crust of your choice. Cut dough and line 12 cups in a muffin pan.

Filling:

Juice of 3 lemons

1 grated lemon rind

¾ cup granulated sugar

5 egg yolks

4 tablespoons melted butter

Mix all ingredients well and fill the shells half full. Bake at

Caramel Corn

400 degrees for 10–20 minutes or until the crust is browning and the filling bubbles.

Meringue:

5 egg whites

½ teaspoon cream of tartar

10 teaspoons granulated sugar

Beat egg whites and cream of tartar until whites are stiff, then slowly add sugar, beating constantly. Beat until smooth and glassy. Remove tarts from oven and add generous spoonfuls to tarts. Bake at 300 degrees for approximately 20 minutes or until meringue is golden brown.

Enjoy!

"Recipes are like poems; they keep what kept us.
And good cooks are like poets; they know how to count."
HENRI COULETTE

Lesson #13
Pass along your best-loved recipes for others to enjoy.

Bert Waugh Jr. *(inspired by the desperate needs of kids living on the streets of Portland, he and his wife, Susy, founded Transitional Youth in 1991)*

Chapter 14

"People will forget what you said, people will forget what you did, but people will never forget how you made them feel."

MAYA ANGELOU

> "How wonderful it is that nobody need wait a single moment before starting to improve the world."
>
> ANNE FRANK

Track Walker

How would you live differently if you knew your heart could fail at any time? How would it affect your attitude on life and others? The next funeral I attended was held for "Neil" at a large Presbyterian church in the Portland suburbs. The moment I started hearing the eulogies, I understood how Neil made the choice to live. He was born with transposition of the great vessels; the aorta and the pulmonary artery were switched and he had a hole in his heart. The doctors told his parents when he was two days old that he would not live for very long; he made it to forty-five.

Interestingly, Neil's family doctor gave one of the eulogies. It was the only service I went to where a representative from the hospital spoke. I was moved by the relationship Neil and his doctor had. He started off by saying how many people from the hospital wished they could have been there and how Neil had made an impact on them; he named over fifteen individuals. The doctor talked about the positive power Neil had when he was there. He stayed positive until his last hours. Neil always focused on his twelve-year-old daughter and the trips he wanted to take her on. He especially wanted to go to Yosemite and live long enough to see his daughter get married.

Neil's doctor went on to paint a picture of Neil's generosity. He spoke of a recent fundraiser held by the American Heart Association, and the Association asked the hospital to get involved. This doctor received an e-mail asking for donations. When he scrolled down the list of donors, he saw Neil's name at the bottom as being the biggest donor with the fewest resources. He quickly matched the donation and motivated his colleagues to do the same.

Neil participated in walks for the American Heart Association with tubes in his nose as he pulled his oxygen tank. How many excuses have we come up with for not making a difference? In the last six months, what have you done for a local charity?

Neil's boss got up and talked about Neil's passion and dedication to work. He never missed a day unless he was in the hospital. Neil also made time to be a volunteer firefighter to help others.

I saw Neil's strength passed down in his young daughter. She stood in front of the group with two other girls and sang with confidence and a smile in memory of her dad.

How would your relationship with your family change if you knew you could die at any moment? This man made every day count. He lived and treated every day as a gift.

What are we waiting for?

One of my clients in Oregon is the retail chain Fred Meyer. I am impressed with the difference they make in the community. They raise money for different groups by way of Relay for Life and other similar events.

The specific store that I worked with is located in Wilsonville, Oregon. The store director, Sam Strouse, is leading his team to make a true difference in the community. They have adopted a road to maintain and clean, have set up a reading program at the local library, feed the seniors once a month, and are heavily involved in the school district. They are a partner with the people in the community.

There are many benefits of doing this besides increasing their business; the store truly connects with the community and understands its needs. Every associate is involved in some way.

What is your company doing to make a difference?

> "The purpose of life is not to be (merely) happy.
> I think the purpose of life is to be useful, to be honorable,
> to be compassionate. I think it is above all to matter, to count,
> to stand for something. To have it make some difference that
> you lived at all."
> LEO ROSTEN

> "Act as if what you do makes a difference. It does."
> WILLIAM JAMES

Lesson #14
For a more fulfilling life,
get involved with at least one charity.

Grant Hammersley *(CEO of Opus Solutions, boater, golfer, Greenbay Packer fan, father, and husband)*

Chapter 15

"Given there are no luggage racks attached to your final day on this great planet, making each day your masterpiece personally and professionally seems to make great sense."

> "Work hard, play hard."
> NIKE SLOGAN

Bagpipers

The next funeral I attended was held at a large nondenominational church in downtown Portland. It was held for "Eric," who had died at the age of eighty-seven, only three months after his wife had died. Eric had emigrated here from Ireland when he was a boy and had been taught to work hard. The church was filled with family who had flown in from Ireland.

Eric's daughter talked about the influence he had had on children. He encouraged them to work hard picking strawberries on their farm so they could save money to travel to Ireland. Eric taught them the lesson of putting in the work and enjoying the reward.

I could see the influence Eric had had on his grandchildren. One grandson played "When Irish Eyes Are Smiling" on the bagpipes; he displayed confidence and pride as he played.

WHEN IRISH EYES ARE SMILING

There's a tear in your eye,
and I'm wondering why,
For it never should be there at all.
With such power in your smile,
sure a stone you'd beguile,

So there's never a teardrop should fall.
When your sweet lilting laughter's like some fairy song,
And your eyes twinkle bright as can be;
You should laugh all the while

And all other times smile,
And now, smile a smile for me.

When Irish eyes are smiling,
Sure 'tis like the morn in Spring.
In the lilt of Irish laughter,
You can hear the angels sing.
When Irish hearts are happy,
All the world seems bright and gay.
And when Irish eyes are smiling,
Sure, they steal your heart away.

This song was written by Chauncey Olcott and George Graff Jr. in 1912 and set to music by Ernest Ball. The message is be happy, smile, and find laughter!

Here is an example of creating a fun workplace that I think is interesting. I hope you do, too. The company referred to in the article is Goodmortgage.com, an online mortgage lender in Charlotte, North Carolina.

The Charlotte-based company is one of the area's fastest-growing entrepreneurial firms. But it's also growing a reputation with employees for little extras, including birthday cake, free sodas, wear-shorts-to-work days, and video games and ping-pong tables in the break room. Founder and chief executive Keith Luedeman says these small extras and a full suite of traditional benefits help the company attract top young talent and build rapport among sixty-two employees.

"People are so much more productive when they're happy," says Luedeman, wearing khaki shorts and a Hawaiian shirt on a recent Friday afternoon. Luedeman designed renovations at the former warehouse to support a work-hard/play-hard atmosphere. Cubicles are surrounded by common areas that foster camaraderie and relieve stress. A large lounge is stocked with free sodas, hot beverages, and candy bars. An adjacent common area boasts HD TVs and video-game consoles. A basketball court and fitness center—complete with free weights and iPod docking stations—takes up one wing of the building. The company allows employees to use the facilities before and after work or during short breaks throughout the day as a way to alleviate work-related stress. Every employee receives a cake and balloons on his birthday. Parking spaces, free lunches, and plaques are awarded regularly to high achievers (O'Daniel 2010).

"Surround yourself with people who take their work seriously, but not themselves, those who work hard and play hard."
COLIN POWELL

Lesson #15
Work hard so you can play hard.

Patrick Galvin *(chief galvinizer for Galvin Communications, fluent in three languages)*

Chapter 16

"I've visited more than forty countries and every continent except Africa. I'm addicted to travel because I'm intensely curious to learn how others live. My trips have played an integral role in the development of a deep-seated gratitude for what I have and what I can give back as a husband, father, son, brother, and citizen of the world."

> "The world is a book and those who do not travel read only one page."
>
> St. Augustine

World Map

This is the only service I went to where I had previously met the deceased, "Michael." He had attended a graduation of someone I had taught, demonstrating his loyalty for others. Michael's service was a graveside ceremony at a cemetery located directly between my home and work. I was disappointed with myself that I had driven by this graveyard hundreds of times and never noticed it, being too into my own world.

This time was different because the friend I was with introduced me to his friends and I heard stories about Michael before the service. They talked about their trips to France with him. They talked about his confidence and love for travel. They told a story about how Michael didn't care what others thought and sported a Speedo at the pool.

As the service started, I was staring at the pictures of Michael and his map of the world. He had red tacks on all the places he had traveled to. He had traveled the world, lived in Paris, and was fluent in French. Michael's niece spoke about what fun memories she had of her uncle. She described him as smart, generous, and always challenging people.

A family friend talked about his passion for all the places Michael had lived, including Oregon, New York, and France. She held up *The World Almanac* and talked about how he loved facts and learning. Other friends said that Michael was a fascinating conversationalist and they always learned from him. He was constantly staying current with the news by reading the *New York Times* daily. Once, Michael was invited to go to a Portland Trail Blazer game and he had to ask what a rebound was. He knew all the stats for every player before he arrived at the game. He had a thirst for knowledge and was constantly learning.

Michael's passion and desire for travel hit me the most. On his picture board he had many photos of him traveling with a genuine smile. Michael died suddenly in June and had trips booked in August and September. He was eighty-two when he died and was going to travel until the very last day.

I have a map in my kitchen with all the places I have been. It is the tabletop on our table. It is a wonderful visual to remember where I have been and what my next adventure will be!

Others also share my zest for travel. LoadSpring Solutions, an enterprise software company, believes people grow by experiencing other cultures. Employees who travel abroad for vacation receive up to five thousand dollars toward their expenses and an extra week off to expand their horizons (Blue 2011).

> "If you want to succeed you should strike out on new paths, rather than travel the worn paths of accepted success."
> JOHN D. ROCKEFELLER

> "Just to travel is rather boring, but to travel with a purpose is educational and exciting."
> SARGENT SHRIVER

In ancient Rome, when a victorious general paraded through the streets, legend has it that he was trailed by a servant whose job it was to repeat to him, "Memento mori": Remember you will die. A reminder of mortality would help the hero keep things in perspective, instill some humility. Jobs's memento mori had been delivered by the doctors, but it did not instill humility. Instead he roared back after his recovery with even more passion. The illness reminded him that he had nothing to lose, so he should forge ahead full speed (Isaacson 461).

What places will you explore and how will that change you?

> **Lesson #16**
> Travel to expand your horizons.

Timothy Birr *(A retired firefighter, plays the pipes at the Oregon Irish Famine Memorial. A piper since 1967, Tim helped start the Tualatin Valley Fire & Rescue Pipes and Drums in 2000 as a way of bringing an element of tradition into fire service functions and ceremonies.)*

Chapter 17

"Tradition connects us with our past, and provides context for our future."

> "What an enormous magnifier is tradition!
> How a thing grows in the human memory
> and in the human imagination, when love,
> worship, and all that lies in the human
> heart, is there to encourage it."
>
> THOMAS CARLYLE

Candles and Incense

This was one of only three services where I was asked what I was doing there. I was intrigued by the obituary for this sixty-five-year-old Vietnamese woman, "Huong," who had come to the United States when she was a young girl. I entered the funeral home and sat in the back waiting for the funeral to start. Fifteen minutes had gone by and nothing was happening. Seven other people, who I assumed to be family members, all sat in the front row, their heads bowed. Each family member wore a white mourning band around his/her left arm. I saw that sticks of incense had been placed on a table near the casket. After a few minutes, one of the family members walked over to me and asked if he could help me. I told him that I was there to observe and that everything was beautiful. He smiled and said thank you.

I stayed for about fifteen minutes longer and observed what people did. Individuals or small groups of people entered and walked directly to the front; they looked in the casket, lit incense, and sat and talked with the family for a few minutes. There was no program and no service as such. The "service" was just private time with the family. Though sad, the atmosphere felt peaceful and calm. There was a relaxed feeling that allowed people to really connect.

When I got home from the funeral, I read online about the traditions of different cultures and funerals. While researching Vietnamese funeral customs, I read,

"The sense of the dead is that of the final," says a Vietnamese proverb, implying that funeral ceremonies must be solemnly organized.

Formerly, funerals went as follows: the body was washed and dressed, a chopstick was laid between the teeth, and then a pinch of rice and three coins were dropped in the mouth.

The body was laid on a grass mat spread on the ground, enveloped with white cloth, and put into a coffin. Finally, the funeral ceremony was officially performed. The coffin is buried and covered, but after three days of mourning, the family visits the tomb again and opens the grave for worship. Finally, after forty-nine days, the family stops bringing rice for the dead to the altar. And then, after one hundred days, the family celebrates *tot khoc*, or the end of the tears.

After one year there is a ceremony for the first anniversary of the relative's death and after two years in the end of mourning festival.

Nowadays, morning ceremonies follow new rituals that are simplified; they consist of covering and putting the dead body into the coffin, the funeral procession, the burial of the coffin into the grave, and the visits to the tomb. The deceased's family members wear a white turban or a black mourning band (Source: http://www.vietnam-culture.com/articles-22-3/Funeral-ceremonies.aspx).

There is always some type of funeral ceremony and ritual, a sacred place for the dead and a way to memorialize the dead. Everyone does it in their own way that brings the closure they need. Tradition plays a big part of bringing people together to bond with each other.

Many companies have traditions that bridge the gap between staff of differing seniority. When people celebrate and participate in the traditions at the job, they make work a better place. Pumpkin carving contests at Halloween, company picnics in the summer, and holiday parties are a few events that associates look forward to.

One of my clients, Opus Solutions, has a tradition of taking their team to a mountain retreat at Black Butte Ranch as a team-building exercise. I worked with them on their presentation skills at one of their off-site meetings and saw the benefit of getting away from the office. Changing the environment helps people connect and discover their more personal sides.

What do your associates look forward to, and how can you make lasting memories with them?

"Traditions are the guideposts driven deep in our subconscious minds. The most powerful ones are those we can't even describe, aren't even aware of."
ELLEN GOODMAN

"Family traditions counter alienation and confusion. They help us define who we are; they provide something steady, reliable, and safe in a confusing world."
SUSAN LIEBERMAN

Lesson #17
Honor your traditions.

Mindy Mayer *(plane crash survivor who lost five of her closest family members in August 2007 on a floatplane crash in Alaska)*

Chapter 18

"You can either lie down or move forward as the choice is yours—I chose to live my life to the fullest for all of those family members that are no longer around to do so."

> "Dream as if you'll live forever,
> live as if you'll die today."
> JAMES DEAN

Steelhead

There were about sixty people at this service for "Jake," who had died at the age of fifty-seven. It was held in the same little church that he and his wife had been married in. Most of the people seemed to have been from his work and the church. Jake was described by his friends as honest, brave, and passionate. They had us close our eyes and scroll through our memories of this man and the stories we remembered. I was disappointed that only four people spoke; there were so many memories to tell to help the family on that day.

Jake's brother and sister told many stories about getting in trouble as children. They told a story about how Jake had brought a hose into their house for a water fight and other ways they challenged their single mom. As they told these stories, I watched their mom. She was laughing and smiling, hearing the stories.

Some coworkers told stories about how Jake organized a fishing trip every Thanksgiving morning to catch steelhead. He had a true passion for the outdoors and fishing. He never missed that Thanksgiving tradition with friends. His passion came from being raised on the Oregon coast where he grew up with sport of fishing.

Jake's loved ones encouraged us to live life a little more, for this was a reminder about how quickly life goes by.

We all have a catalog of pictures and memories of our life. What do we choose to focus on and remember? Do we take opportunities to remind ourselves of what we have accomplished? Do we only look at the past and stop making changes to live today?

My friend Megan Garcia gave me the book *If I Had My Life to Live Over I Would Pick More Daisies* (Martz 1992) in 1994 and wrote, "Thanks for picking daisies with me!" I especially liked this poem by eighty-five-year-old Nadine Stair that was included and think of it often:

If I Had My Life to Live Over

I'd dare to make more mistakes next time. I'd relax, I would limber up. I would be sillier than I have been this trip. I would take fewer things seriously. I would take more chances. I would climb more mountains and swim more rivers. I would eat more ice cream and less beans. I would perhaps have more actual troubles, but I'd have fewer imaginary ones.

You see, I'm one of those people who live sensibly and sanely, hour after hour, day after day. Oh, I've had my moments, and if I had to do it over again, I'd have more of them. In fact, I'd try to have nothing else. Just moments, one after another, instead of living so many years ahead of each day. I've been one of those persons who never goes anywhere without a thermometer, a hot water bottle, a raincoat, and a parachute. If I had to do it again, I would travel lighter than I have.

If I had my life to live over, I would start barefoot earlier in the spring and stay that way later in the fall. I would go to more dances. I would ride more merry-go-rounds. I would pick more daisies.

How can you live life a little more today?

"Nobody can go back and start a new beginning, but anyone can start today and make a new ending."
MARIA ROBINSON

"When life gives you a hundred reasons to cry, show life that you have a thousand reasons to smile."
AUTHOR UNKNOWN

Lesson #18
Appreciate every precious day of your life.

Bill Bezio with Kyle and Mackenzie (devoted father and husband)

Chapter 19

"They say that time is money. Well it may not be the kind of money we can pay our bills with, but it is definitely one of the most valuable assets we possess. As I think of my children's future and how my wife and I will pay for their college education, their weddings, their personal growth, the best *investment* I can make in them is my time! Not just paying attention to them, but . . . making an emotional connection and truly appreciating their ideas, opinions, and commentary on life. I believe it helps them develop a healthy self-worth . . . from which to grow and mature into well rounded and self-confident grown-ups."

> "Time is what we want most,
> but what we use worst."
> WILLIAM PENN

Family Man

The next funeral I attended was held for a man, "Mark," who had lived a long, full life. I walked into the service at the large Universalist church and went straight back to the right side of the room. Orange chairs lined the back of the church; I chose one next to a man. I got out the program and read it about fifteen times until the service started. There were many children at this service; extra chairs were added to accommodate the two hundred people who were there.

We all stood and sang "Amazing Grace." After that, the story of Mark's life began to unfold. He had lived in California as a child and met his wife on the farm where he worked. They were married sixty-nine years! Mark was described as a hardworking man who had served in World War II as a police officer. Mark was very well known and respected in his industry in Portland. He had passed his trade to his sons, teaching them the business. They told stories about how Mark loved to work in his shop for hours as his hobby. People brought their cars to him and he fixed them for free because of his passion to help others.

It was evident that family was Mark's passion. He and his wife had had five children, twenty-eight grandchildren, eight great-grandchildren, and five great-great-grandchildren. Loved ones told many stories about him making paper boats to float down the river, catching crayfish, fishing, and laughing with his children and grandchildren.

One of Mark's granddaughters spoke about her appreciation for her grandparents. They were the role models for how to love and to be good people. She told us that Mark had once described his wife as 90 percent of the glue that kept the family together. As I watched the slideshow, I could see evidence of that. They included a picture of Mark and his wife in his last days; his wife had her hand lovingly on him, dedicated for sixty-nine years.

Mark died at the age of eighty-nine while receiving hospice care in his home. His helpers positioned his bed so he could look out the window and watch his family—his true love and source of happiness.

The Oregon National Guard ended the service with "Taps" played on a trumpet. They folded the flag from the casket and presented it to his wife as they whispered something in her ear.

Mark had influenced many and brought much happiness to children by being active in their lives, listening, and truly loving life.

When I attended the National Speakers Association meeting in Florida in 2010, I had the honor of hearing Wintley Phipps sing "Amazing Grace." The story behind the song intrigued me.

Wintley Phipps Says:

"A lot of people don't realize that just about all Negro spirituals are written on the black notes of the piano. Probably the most famous on this slave scale was written by John Newton, who used to be the captain of a slave ship, and many believe he heard this melody that sounds very much like a West African sorrow chant. And it has a haunting, haunting plaintive quality to it that reaches past your arrogance, past your pride, and it speaks to that part of you that's in bondage. And we feel it. We feel it. It's just one of the most amazing melodies in all of human history."

It is amazing to think that there are eighty-eight keys on the piano and that famous song uses less than thirty-six. How many keys are you using in your life? How could you make your life more meaningful?

"If we take care of the moments,
the years will take care of themselves."
MARIA EDGEWORTH

"If you want to make good use of your time, you've got to know what's most important and then give it all you've got."
LEE IACOCCA

Lesson #19
Give to others your time and attention.

Josh Oller *(volunteer for Search One K-9 Detection, father, husband, and owner of the Silver Lining Jewelry and Loan)*

Chapter 20

"A true measurement of success in life is when you can look back on all that you have done for others."

> "Never look down on anybody
> unless you're helping him up."
>
> JESSE JACKSON

Rocks

The next funeral I attended was for a sixty-nine-year-old man, "Jeff," who had grown up in Honolulu, Hawaii. When I entered the funeral home, there were many people wearing leis and floral dresses and shirts. They described Jeff as a man with passion for the water and said he was a true lifeguard. Friends of Jeff's related the challenging way that he, a pastoral counselor, interacted with others. They said he often let people struggle a bit and when they truly needed help, he would be there for them. He challenged others to discover answers themselves.

One of Jeff's friends told the story that Jeff would tell others about the futility of worrying. He told people to imagine throwing a rock into the ocean. The rock will land at the bottom. He then asked people what will happen if they try to swim after the rock; the answer is that they will drown. Jeff encouraged others to think of their worries that were out of their control as rocks. Throw the rock—your worry—into the ocean and let it go. There is nothing that we can do about the past and we are wasting our energy by worrying about it.

By listening and coaching others to discover their own answers, Jeff left a positive imprint before he died. They used Mother Theresa's words at Jeff's service: "In this life we cannot do great things. We can only do small things with great love."

As I drove home from the funeral, I thought of my own situation. Two years ago, I fell deeply in love and, for the first time, became vulnerable and really open to someone. The timing in life was not right and I broke off the relationship. That person meant the world to me. He treated me like a queen but I was not ready to commit. After we had broken up, he made a choice that upset me for over a year. I reflected on the wasted negative emotion and energy I chose to use. I wish I had taken the advice of this lifeguard and written my problem on a rock and thrown it in into the Columbia River in Portland. Life is short and we choose how we spend our time and emotions.

Is there something from your past that you are not releasing? The only thing we have control of is the present. So often we do not forgive and let go. I challenge you to write down three things that you need to release and let go.

1.

2.

3.

Find a rock, write the items on it, find some deep water, and release the rock. This is a visual that you have no control over. Change that energy into something positive and that you can control. When you do, you will be less stressed and more focused on the positive parts of life.

"To forgive is the highest, most beautiful form of love. In return, you will receive untold peace and happiness."
Robert Muller

"Once again I heard that cold, steady voice in my head rise above the emotional chaos. *Look forward*, it said. *Save your strength for the things you can change. If you cling to the past, you will die.*"

NANDO PARRADO
of his survival following a plane crash in the Andes Mountains (2006, 75)

Lesson #20
Be a lifeguard to others; stop negative situations.

Lessons We've Learned

11 Connect with many people through a balanced life.

12 Remember that you are loved and make a difference to many people.

13 Pass along your best-loved recipes for others to enjoy.

14 For a more fulfilling life, get involved with at least one charity.

15 Work hard so you can play hard.

16 Travel to expand your horizons.

17 Honor your traditions.

18 Appreciate every precious day of your life.

19 Give to others your time and attention.

20 Be a lifeguard to others; stop negative situations.

Gerard McAleese—Kells Irish Restaurant & Pub *(immigrated to the United States from Ireland in 1980 and opened the first Kells in Seattle in 1983)*

Chapter 21

"I opened up a Irish bar/restaurant because I am proud of where I am from. The Irish culture, the music and dancing, is all part of the 'crack' fun and laughter. I started Kells because I wanted to show people in America there was more to an Irish bar than paper shamrocks and green beer. If you can't go to Ireland, come to Kells!"

> "Success is not the result of spontaneous combustion. You must set yourself on fire."
>
> FRED SHERO

Sail Away

I Hope You Dance

Written by Tia Sillers, Mark D. Sanders

I hope you never lose your sense of wonder
You get your fill to eat but always keep that hunger
May you never take one single breath for granted
God forbid love ever leave you empty-handed
I hope you still feel small when you stand beside the ocean
Whenever one door closes I hope one more opens
Promise me that you'll give faith a fighting chance
And when you get the choice to sit it out or dance

I hope you dance
I hope you dance

I hope you never fear those mountains in the distance
Never settle for the path of least resistance
Livin' might mean takin' chances, but they're worth takin'
Lovin' might be a mistake, but it's worth makin'
Don't let some Hellbent heart leave you bitter
When you come close to sellin' out, reconsider

Give the heavens above more than just a passing glance
And when you get the choice to sit it out or dance

I hope you dance
I hope you dance
(Time is a wheel in constant motion always rolling us along)
I hope you dance
I hope you dance
(Tell me who wants to look back on their years and wonder,
where those years have gone?)

I hope you still feel small when you stand beside the ocean
Whenever one door closes I hope one more opens
Promise me that you'll give faith a fighting chance
And when you get the choice to sit it out or dance

Dance
(Time is a wheel in constant motion always rolling us along)
I hope you dance
I hope you dance
(Tell me who wants to look back on their years and wonder,
where those years have gone?)

Reading the obituaries became a daily activity for me. I read about interesting people. Just as companies read résumés, I selected the services I would attend by their life facts. One obituary in the Sunday paper really caught my attention.

The deceased person, a woman named "Joan," was described as having sparkling eyes, a ready smile, and an open heart, and as the first one on the dance floor when the music started. I knew I had to attend this one because I love to dance and am also one of the first to dance.

Many friends and family members stood at the podium to tell Joan's story. She was one of eight children and had grown up farming. She had met her husband on the farm and dedicated her life to raising

Sail Away

their family. Joan had a passion for sailing and enjoyed the waters of Washington, Canada, and Alaska in a custom sailboat she and her husband had built. Joan's friends related how, in her final years, these memories kept her positive and smiling.

Joan's grandson told a story about two boats in the dock. One was leaving and one coming in. The one that was leaving got all the attention. Really the one that just came in should have received the attention. That boat had survived the storms, turbulence, and adventures. Joan's grandson used this as an analogy for babies and death. We should celebrate when people leave; they have lived a full life and we can remember their adventures. Joan had lived ninety-six years.

At the end of Joan's celebration, the pastor talked about her passion for music and dancing. The church was filled with people from her retirement community. When the pianist played "You Are My Sunshine," described as Joan's favorite song, I saw the sanctuary light up with energy. One by one, the people started to do a slight head shake, and then their bodies came to life, clapping their hands and tapping their walkers and canes. The energy and passion in the room was contagious. People were laughing and smiling. It was the last impression they would have of this woman. What a gift to leave people with.

What gift are you leaving people? Do you really see all your strengths? Write your top ten strengths and ten people you have influenced. Reflect on your strengths and challenge yourself to mentor and influence more people.

Strengths

1.

2.

3.

4.

5.

6.

7.

8.

9.

10.

People You Have Influenced

1.

2.

3.

4.

5.

6.

7.

8.

9.

10.

Lesson #21
Focus on your strengths and go dance!

Dave Harkin *(marathoner, coach, mentor and co-owner of Portland Running Company with his wife, Paula)*

Chapter 22

"A great performance is 90 percent preparation and 10 percent truth. This truth resides in a private place exposed only at one's weakest moments. This truth resides in overcoming the fear of failure. It is during these moments when the gap between a dream and an accomplishment is bridged. At some point in a marathon, everyone questions how they will finish and why they are even doing a marathon in the first place. There is no earthly answer. That is why it's called the 'moment of truth.'"

> "I've always thought that people need to feel good about themselves and I see my role as offering support to them, to provide some light along the way."
>
> — LEO BUSCAGLIA

What's Wonderful?

As I drove up on a Friday at 5:00 PM, the parking lot was packed. I was attending a late-day funeral at a Lutheran church for a seventy-year-old woman by the name of "Lori." Her six grandchildren were the greeters at the door. I signed the guest book and took my usual seat at the back of the church. There were ten people in the choir along with an organ and piano. We began with "Amazing Grace" and then watched Lori's slideshow. "You Are So Beautiful," "Wind Beneath My Wings," and "Somewhere Over the Rainbow" played. The slideshow featured a lot of pictures of children and grandchildren.

Lori had raised her three children as a single mother and always thought of others first. Lori's daughter, "Kelsey," told one story about Lori's support of Kelsey's running goals. Every day, Lori picked up her grandkids at 6:00 AM with donuts ready and took care of them while Kelsey ran nine miles.

Lori's grandsons told stories about her teaching them to be strong. One time when the car broke down, she pushed it as her eleven-year-old grandson steered the car. Lori always helped others find solutions to their problems. She was always there to listen and stayed positive. She often asked the question, "What wonderful thing happened today?"

Speakers told stories about Lori's calmness when her house was on fire and her loyalty to her friends. Her coworkers talked about her ability to keep her team going. She would say, "Let's just start it!"

Lori's main passion was her family and friends. She loved organizing events like family reunions, outings with friends, and community functions. She sacrificed her time to make others happy. She truly *lived* until she died. Family flew in from all over to celebrate her life and the impact she had made on so many.

In thinking about Lori, the lesson of goal setting came to mind. When is the last time you set goals and wrote a vision statement? Every year I take time to set goals in eight areas of my life: Work, Financial Health, Family, Friends and Fun, Community, Spiritual Health, Physical Health, and Personal Growth. I write eight to ten actions I want to complete in every area. I hold myself accountable to make it happen. Take time now to look at your life and challenge yourself to set goals.

Work Goals:
(Example: Send ten handwritten notes to clients.)
1.

2.

3.

Financial Health Goals:
(Example: Meet with a financial planner.)
1.

2.

3.

Family Goals:
(Example: Plan a fun Sunday dinner.)
1.

2.

3.

Friends and Fun Goals:
(Example: Take a trip to the beach.)
1.

2.

3.

Community Goals:
(Example: Volunteer at the hospital.)
1.

2.

3.

Spiritual Health Goals:
(Example: Meditate for ten minutes every evening.)
1.

2.

3.

Physical Health Goals:
(Example: Take a walk every day.)
1.

2.

3.

Personal Growth Goals:
(Example: Take a dance class.)
1.

2.

3.

After you have written down your goals, look at the next three months and decide what you will make happen. Make sure your goals are attainable.

"Leaders don't create followers, they create more leaders."
TOM PETERS

"The greatest good you can do for another is not just to share your riches but to reveal to him his own."
BENJAMIN DISRAELI

Lesson #22
Help others to reach their goals.

Marshall Nash *(die-hard biker for over thirty years)*

Chapter 23

"We work our whole life for the American dream. The question is, what is the American dream? You know we only get one chance at this world, so I would hope we all find our passion in this life and fire it up!!!"

> "And in the end, it's not the years in your life that count. It's the life in your years."
>
> ABRAHAM LINCOLN

Fresh Raspberries and Ice Cream

The next funeral I attended, in a large Pentecostal church in Portland, was definitely one of the saddest. It was held for a woman, "Eileen," age fifty-six, who had tragically died in a car crash. She had been on her way to a restaurant to celebrate her twenty-eighth wedding anniversary. The church was packed with over one hundred and fifty people, and twenty family members came down the aisle before the service started.

As the mic opened up, stories began to paint a picture of this loving and affectionate woman. The way Eileen would look at her husband, people could tell they were in love after almost thirty years. She made people feel important with her hugs and attention.

Eileen's passions included travel, tennis, singing, and people. She had a gift for making people feel welcome with generosity. Eileen often invited people over to her home. Family members talked about the fresh raspberries and ice cream she would serve her guests.

Eileen died celebrating something she loved more than anything—her marriage to her husband, "David." One story was told about a time that her husband was singing a solo and the audience looked over and saw her watching David with a look of extraordinary loving pride.

How many times have you felt that important in the eyes of a significant other? Do we make others feel important? How do we make others happy? How do we show it with our body language?

On your final exit, what do you want to be doing and who do you want to be with?

Who:

What:

When is the last time you made a loved one feel important? Are you making time for the important people in your life?

During the service, I noticed that some people looked surprised to learn about the love and affection in Eileen's life and the joy she found in singing. How well do you know others in your world? What questions can you ask them to discover more? Make time for people! Stop saying, "One day . . . Someday . . . I should . . ." Do it now! We never know how we will spend our last day.

"You don't get to choose how you are going to die or when.
You can only decide how you're going to live."
JOAN BAEZ

Lesson #23
Make time for the important people in your life.

Joan Monen *(owner of the Wild Hare restaurant, mother, wife, and passionate Canby community member)*

Chapter 24

"As a mother of three children, I understand I am the biggest influence of their behavior and attitude toward life. I want to instill in them that creating a thriving community is good for ALL involved and not just what's good for them!"

> "Children will not remember you for the material things you provided but for the feeling that you cherished them."
> RICHARD L. EVANS

Cheerleader

The next funeral I attended was held in a small rural church for a woman, "Shirley," who had lived eighty years. This was a smaller service of about forty people. There were five flower arrangements on the casket with music piped into the church. Shirley had devoted her life to her children. All the stories told were about her volunteer work with the PTA and Boy Scouts and supporting and cheering on her four boys.

As we watched the slideshow, we saw many pictures of Shirley with her sons and her grandchildren. Her nephew spoke about their relationship and her sense of humor. Shirley took and lived each day one at time. Her passion and focus was always children.

Remember the impact we can have on children. Many companies have programs in place through which employees make time to read with students. Make time to volunteer, listen, and mentor others. When we do, we make a difference in someone's life.

> "Don't worry that children never listen to you; worry that they are always watching you."
> ROBERT FULGHUM

"Children are like wet cement.
Whatever falls on them makes an impression."
Dr. Haim Ginott

Nando Parrado wrote about making his final climb down the mountains after seventy-two days of being in the Andes.

> The mountains, for all their power, were not stronger than my attachment to my father. They could not crush my ability to love. I felt a moment of calmness and clarity, and in that clarity of mind I discovered a simple, astounding secret: Death has an opposite, but the opposite is not mere living. It is not courage or faith or human will. The opposite of death is love. How had I missed that? How does anyone miss that? Love is our only weapon. Only love can turn mere life into a miracle and draw precious meaning from suffering and fear. For a brief and magical moment, all my fears lifted, and I knew that I would not let death control me. I would walk through the godforsaken country that separated me from my home with love and hope in my heart (Parrado 2006, 201).

Lesson #24
Spend time with children.

Becky Mathis *(hairstylist since 1992)*

Chapter 25

"We all have a voice and want to be heard and my job allows me to be the ear for many."

> "We have two ears and one mouth so that we can listen twice as much as we speak."
>
> EPICTETUS

The Photograph

The next service was held for the youngest person whose funeral I attended. The woman, "Melissa," had only been thirty-five years old. Melissa had taken her own life, which I only discovered once I arrived. As I entered the sanctuary of the large Baptist church, it was filled with parents from Melissa's children's school. She had two children who were six and two years old.

There was a blown-up photo of this beautiful woman at the front of the church that I stared at for an hour. All the stories revolved around Melissa's passion for her children, volunteering at the animal clinic, and love for her family. There were many people there to show support. I kept looking at Melissa's distraught husband and children, wondering what they must be experiencing.

The pastor talked about how depression can affect people in ways that we can't understand. I couldn't help but wonder: out of all those people who were at the service, couldn't one person have asked Melissa a question or been more in tune with her?

We have lost so much of the human touch with technology. A friend of mine lost his brother-in-law in a car crash. He put an "out of office" reply on his e-mail for two weeks. He told me later that no one called him during that time to ask if there was a problem. It probably never occurs to us to ask. After all, when someone's out of the office, we usually assume they're on vacation. This experience really woke me up to the reality that I was really in a bubble, not being as connected with people as I could be.

Listening is not innate or automatic; it is a skill we learn through discipline and is the key to effective communication. Hearing and listening are different. Hearing is the process of the physical sound waves entering our ears. Listening is when we interpret, evaluate, and react. Talkers are easy to find; to be a good listener is unique and necessary.

ACC's (Allison Clarke Consulting's) Top 10 Actions to Become a Better Listener:

1. Stop. Drop. Goal. (Stop what you're doing. Drop your cell phone or other distraction, and you will hit your Goal of being an attentive listener.)

2. Choose your environment. (Decide where the best place to have the conversation is.)

3. Look at the speaker.

4. Turn off your thoughts and concentrate on the speaker.

5. Use open body language.

6. Restate words and messages when appropriate.

7. Ask open-ended questions.

8. Train your eyes to look for nonverbal signals.

9. Be patient. Let the other person finish his/her comment.

10. Remind yourself that time and attention to others are important.

The Photograph

"Courage is what it takes to stand up and speak; courage is also what it takes to sit down and listen."
WINSTON CHURCHILL

> **Lesson #25**
> Take time to listen—really listen—to other people.

Melissa Maag *(friend, and mother of two)*

Chapter 26

"I feel there is an unexpected joy that will inevitably flourish from the exchange of a smile with anyone. It is rare that anything but feelings of connection, happiness, and peace manifest from a stranger's smile. Each day my intent is to remember that the small things, smiles being one, bring about a chain of kindness with exponential impact. And to be honest . . . the exchange of a smile with a stranger is not wholly altruistic. The ripple effect for each party and those they encounter is incalculable."

"A smile confuses an approaching frown."
AUTHOR UNKNOWN

Smile

The next service was one of my favorite celebrations of life. It was a small service of about forty-five people in an older church—I believe it was a Primitive Baptist church—with ceiling fans running full blast. The funeral was held for ninety-year-old "Julie" and was upbeat rather than sad.

As I began to understand who Julie was, I admired her strength and attitude. Friends and family told stories about her way of adding value to others' lives. For the last eight years of Julie's life, she was without her physical sight. She had to depend on others for transportation as well as many other aspects of life.

The driver of the wheelchair-accessible van that Julie used for transportation attended the service and related how much he liked Julie and would miss her beautiful smile.

There are many things out of our control in our world. One thing that we can control is our attitude. We choose every day how we act. At the end of Julie's life, when her independence and sight were taken from her, she chose to be positive and make others smile.

Music was a highlight at this celebration. I was inspired by the soloist. He was ninety-two and full of life! Seeing his passion for Julie paired with his love of singing made an impact on us. His enthusiasm encouraged us to sing along when he sang the refrain of "In the Sweet By and By."

The last person to talk was Julie's son. He spoke of her volunteering commitment to the community and to always making others happy. He also said that he was very thankful that Julie taught him how to make her apple pie. She knew where to put her energy.

Every day ask yourself, "How can I add value to other's life and make them smile?" At the end of the day, give yourself the smile test; reflect on how many people had a better day because of your attitude and actions.

Do people smile—or frown—when they see you coming?

"Attitude is a little thing that makes a big difference."
WINSTON CHURCHILL

"Every time you smile at someone, it is an action of love, a gift to that person, a beautiful thing."
MOTHER TERESA

Lesson #26
Smile often to improve your "face" value.

Tricia Rogers *(speech-language pathologist and owner of All About Speech, Inc., started in 2000 to a make a difference for children)*

Chapter 27

"Everyone wears a sign that says 'I want to feel important.' My hope is to make it happen for each and every person I have the pleasure to meet. It also brings me great joy in return."

> "Class is an aura of confidence that is being sure without being cocky. Class has nothing to do with money. Class never runs scared. It is self-discipline and self-knowledge. It is the sure-footedness that comes with having proved you can meet life."
>
> ANN LANDERS

Zip-a-Dee-Doo-Dah

I chose the next funeral because of the tone of the obituary, which was unusually upbeat. The service was held at a large Presbyterian church in Portland and, according to the obituary, would be a huge celebration of "Gretchen's" life. Her life had ended at the age of sixty-five after a fierce battle with cancer. When I found the church and parked, I saw that the parking lot was already in celebration mode. There were over fifty custom and hot rod cars all shiny and colorful, empty and parked. Gretchen's energy was felt before I entered the church filled with over four hundred people.

At most of the celebrations that I attended I got a feeling for who the person was. People's friends are a reflection of who they are. There was a buzz of excitement in the packed church; they were ready to celebrate their friend's life.

Gretchen had worked in a variety of industries and her last one had been with her husband coordinating car shows. Several people spoke about her influence on the industry. One man stood up and pointed to the ten beautiful flower arrangements on the stage. He said that they represented Gretchen's life. She brought class and hospitality to every event, always making people feel important.

The slideshow represented exactly how Gretchen lived life. We listened to upbeat music as many photos flashed by with her laughing and traveling to Asia and Europe, and on cruises all over enjoying people. This celebration gets the Best Open Mic Award. A great many people told stories. One of Gretchen's high school teachers—who was ninety-two—was there and told us what a joy Gretchen had been as a student.

A childhood friend told us how Gretchen had sung "Zip-a-Dee-Doo-Dah" in fifth grade and it really represented her. Gretchen had been a Zip-a-Dee-Doo-Dah type of woman! Another man took the mic and confessed that he had always had a crush on Gretchen since high school, making everyone laugh. Her cousin spoke of fun road trips to Vegas.

Gretchen's obituary said that she loved life and was active throughout hers with organizing gatherings and good-time get-togethers for classmates, club members, and neighborhood associations. Her social circle grew with each and every endeavor. She was remarkable and memorable.

What type of memories do you leave with people? How can you bring class to situations to make people feel important? Will your teachers speak at your celebration? What will your slideshow be filled with?

Are you laughing, playing, and enjoying life enough? What else can you do today to make that happen?

"Self-praise is for losers. Be a winner.
Stand for something. Always have class and be humble."
JOHN MADDEN

Lesson #27
Approach life with class and you'll never go wrong.

Sharon Murphy *(director of PAWS Animal Shelter, opened in June 1999, she has saved thousands of cats and other animals)*

Chapter 28

"This is the place where happy endings begin."

> "Until one has loved an animal, a part of one's soul remains unawakened."
>
> ANATOLE FRANCE

Animal Lover

For this funeral service, held for "Sally," the Lutheran church was filled with many of her classmates from school as well as friends from the community. Throughout Sally's seventy-one years, I could tell, she had many close relationships. Her niece talked about Sally's sense of humor and dedication to her mother. Sally had taken early retirement to take care of her mom so she didn't have to be in a nursing home. She was a very giving person to many.

What passion will you have until the day you die? For Sally, hers was nature and animals. Friends spoke about her involvement with animal rights causes and initiatives.

Many of the celebrations I attended talked about pets or included them in the slideshow. I know the personal difference animals make in my life and there is medical research to back it up.

"Studies have shown that Alzheimer's patients have fewer anxious outbursts if there is an animal in the home," says Lynette Hart, PhD, associate professor at the University of California at Davis School of Veterinary Medicine.

"Their caregivers also feel less burdened when there is a pet, particularly if it is a cat, which generally requires less care than a dog," says Hart.

Walking a dog or just caring for a pet—for elderly people who are able—can provide exercise and companionship. One insurance company, Midland Life Insurance Company of Columbus, Ohio, asks clients over age seventy-five if they have a pet as part of their medical screening—which often helps tip the scales in their favor.

Enjoying nature and the outdoors has many benefits for us too. Tina Vindum wrote an article called "Reduce Stress in the Great Outdoors" on the Athleta Chi web page (2011). Here is what she found:

> Studies have shown that being in a natural, outdoor environment is one of the very best things you can do for your health:
>
> - Levels of serotonin, a neurotransmitter that helps regulate our mood, rises when we are outside. One study found that regular outdoor runners were less anxious and depressed than people who ran indoors on a treadmill, and had higher levels of post-exercise endorphins, the feel-good brain chemicals associated with "runner's high."
>
> - Exposure to nature reduces pain and illness and speeds recovery time. A study of post-operative patients, those who had rooms with a view of natural surroundings needed less pain medication and spent fewer days in the hospital than those who faced a brick wall.
>
> - Research by Dr. David Lewis, the man who coined the term "road rage," found that the scent of grass has a significant calming effect on out-of-control drivers.
>
> - You also do your lungs a favor when you exercise outdoors: According to the Environmental Protection Agency, indoor air in the US is two to five times more polluted than outdoor air (meaning the outdoor air is 75% less polluted than indoor air!). Fresh air is also rich in negative ions (oxygen molecules with an extra electron). These negative ions have been linked to

improved sense of well-being, heightened awareness and alertness, decreased anxiety, and a lower resting heart rate.

Companies like Nike and Columbia Sportswear encourage employees to go outside. When I worked with Columbia Sportswear, I often saw their team members enjoying the outdoor volleyball courts. They also had many organized team opportunities like softball and basketball. When I visited Nike, I was impressed to see that they have a 1.9-mile running trail that goes through a heavily wooded area for their employees.

At the end of Sally's life, her dog and nature added happiness and peace. Let's take time to smell the roses and look at the stars.

"Any glimpse into the life of an animal quickens our own and makes it so much the larger and better in every way."
JOHN MUIR

"Our task must be to free ourselves . . . by widening our circle of compassion to embrace all living creatures and the whole of nature and its beauty."
ALBERT EINSTEIN

Lesson #28
For your own well-being, get outdoors as much as possible.

Jake French—inspirational speaker (in 2008 his life changed when he sustained a devastating spinal cord injury)

Chapter 29

"It takes an incredible amount of courage to look deep inside yourself and identify where your weaknesses are, or what the anchors look like that are holding you back. Embrace this courage and real progress will start to happen."

> "Keep your fears to yourself, but
> share your courage with others."
> ROBERT LOUIS STEVENSON

Courage

The next funeral I attended was held for a forty-nine-year-old woman, "Nancy," who had lost her battle with breast cancer. The service was held at one of the smaller funeral homes in town and was attended by only about forty people, including family. I felt Nancy's strength in her eighteen-year-old daughter, "Alex." Alex first talked about how disappointed she was that her mom couldn't be there to take her shopping or teach her how to cook. As I watched this young woman speak, I saw that her mom had taught her something much more important; she had demonstrated courage.

Alex was the only one brave enough to stand and speak about Nancy. She was confident and well-spoken. In her battle with cancer, Nancy had remained strong and positive for the people around her. She had passed along that ability to Alex. As I left the funeral home, I thought about the courageous people I know and how lucky I am to have them in my world.

I am involved with the Children's Cancer Association as a chemo pal. I have the opportunity to work with children who have cancer. One of my pals was a sixteen-year-old girl, "Zoe." Zoe inspired me every visit by staying positive and having a strong vision of playing basketball and going to prom soon. It was my first experience seeing what really goes on during the chemo process. Zoe's vision came true and she beat cancer, went to prom, and is training for the basketball team. Every time I left after her appointments, I was thankful for my girls' health and happy I could help another family.

To choose to be strong and positive for a healthy person can be challenging. To watch a sick person demonstrate a positive attitude is inspiring. My challenge to you is that when you want to complain about your life, stop and make a list of what you are grateful for. I strongly believe that when we start to look at the positives, we can change our attitudes and outlook.

List twenty things you are grateful for:

1.

2.

3.

4.

5.

6.

7.

8.

9.

10.

11.

12.

13.

14.

Courage

15.

16.

17.

18.

19.

20.

After you have completed this, make a copy and post it somewhere you will see it every day. When you have a challenge, have a hard day, or feel down, look at this list to put life back into to perspective. This will also give you courage when you focus on your positives.

> "Courage is being scared to death but saddling up anyway."
> JOHN WAYNE

> "Leaders are visionaries with a poorly developed sense of fear and no concept of the odds against them."
> ROBERT JARVIK

> "The bravest thing you can do when you are not brave is to profess courage and act accordingly."
> CORRA HARRIS

Lesson #29
Bring your courage to the forefront.

Carol and Justin DeBoer (married in 1969)

Chapter 30

"As a couple we have always been best friends, supporting and loving each other faithfully. We have always had family first in our lives and enjoyed every aspect of life as a couple and family unit. We truly enjoy being together . . . with lots of hugs, smiles, laughter, encouragement, and love!"

> "Whenever you're in conflict with someone, there is one factor that can make the difference between damaging your relationship and deepening it. That factor is attitude."
>
> WILLIAM JAMES

Square Dancer

At the final funeral I attended in sixty days, the minister told us to choose the qualities that we liked about "Patti" and become more of that type of person. Patti had lived to be eighty-seven.

She and her husband had been married for almost seventy years! I watched Patti's husband during the ceremonies and the slideshow. Their pictures reflected their love for one another. Family members talked about how the couple kept the honeymoon alive by appreciating each other daily. They had shared passions like square dancing, bowling, and their grandchildren, great-grandchildren, and great-great-grandchildren.

After the service, I thought about the current state of marriage in America. With the current divorce rate being over 50 percent, how many marriages could have been saved if people felt more appreciated and had more common interests? I don't know the answer; I am among the half that, after eleven years of marriage, got divorced. Attending this funeral made me think of how different relationships are today as compared to fifty years ago. For many people, technology and constant connectivity has actually estranged them from others rather than bringing them closer to the people in their lives.

There are ways we can keep the honeymoon alive in personal relationships and at work. We can make people feel important, add fun to life, and not wait for the holidays to treat people well. Think how much nicer people are during the holiday season. I observe it every year; people engage more with strangers, smile more, and are in a better mood.

Why do we wait to send a card only once a year or get involved in charities for only a month? How can you do something every month to make someone feel important and make a difference now?

When I lived in Smithfield, Virginia, in 1999, I considered writing a book about how to make marriages stay alive. (Maybe I should have, since I divorced in 2008.) I interviewed over twenty-five women and asked for stories to be sent to me. I wanted horror stories as well as what made their marriages work. Every story that I got that told of a positive impact on the relationship was an example of making the other person feel important, from a homemade birthday cake to a toy airplane with a note attached saying her husband had booked a trip for her. The key was doing the little things that most people don't take the time to do.

All the "horror" stories centered on forgetting birthday and events and not giving the hurt party the attention s/he needed or wanted. We all know that people's expectations are very different in every relationship. Wouldn't it save lots of fights, hurt feelings, and possible ending of relationships if we had a clear picture of what the other person needed and wanted?

Just as companies give reviews to their employees, shouldn't relationships be treated the same way? This is a guide I have given to some people as a tool to understand needs of appreciation.

Three reasons I appreciate (Name):

1.

2.

3.

Square Dancer

Write down your expectations for the year. Do this as an exercise right now with your spouse or significant other so s/he understands your expectations.

New Year's Day: *(Example: Watch football.)*
_____

Valentine's Day:
_____

St. Patrick's Day:
_____

Spring Holiday:
_____

Memorial Day:
_____

Summer trips:
_____

Fourth of July:
_____

Labor Day:
_____

Halloween:
_____

Thanksgiving:
_____

Winter Holiday:
_____

Birthday:

_____

Anniversary:

_____

This is a good planning tool for trips and events and appreciation. Even if you don't share the passion for your partner's requests, isn't it worth indulging to make a difference to make a difference to him/her? One of my good friends has a wonderful company, Unforgettable Honeymoons, which plans romantic trips. Check it out: http://www.unforgettablehoneymoons.com/.

Many of my male friends don't get why they have to send flowers or cards, but when they do, they see the results. I had one friend write fifteen qualities he admired about his wife for their fifteenth anniversary. She said it was the best gift she had ever received.

The same thing will work for companies. Do something unique for people on their birthdays and their anniversaries with the company. You will build trust, build loyalty, and show people that you appreciate them.

Upon Nando Parrado's safe return home to his family, he wrote:

> My duty is to fill my time on earth with as much life as possible, to become a little more human every day, and to understand that we only become humans when we love. I have loved, passionately, fearlessly, with all my heart and my soul, and I have been loved in return. For me this is enough (2006, 264).

"Too often we underestimate the power of a touch, a smile, a kind word, a listening ear, an honest compliment, or the smallest act of caring, all of which have the potential to turn a life around."
Leo Buscaglia

"Don't marry the person you think you can live with; marry only the individual you think you can't live without."
James C. Dobson

Lesson #30
Show your loved ones appreciation in special ways.

Lessons We've Learned

21 Focus on your strengths and go dance!

22 Help others to reach their goals.

23 Make time for the important people in your life.

24 Spend time with children.

25 Take time to listen—really listen—to other people.

26 Smile often to improve your "face" value.

27 Approach life with class and you'll never go wrong.

28 For your own well-being, get outdoors as much as possible.

29 Bring your courage to the forefront.

30 Show your loved ones appreciation in special ways.

> "Live as if you were to die tomorrow.
> Learn as if you were to live forever."
>
> MAHATMA GANDHI

Conclusion

Promise me that you will focus on what you have accomplished in life. Think about what people will say about you when your day comes to leave this world. What do you want to change, explore, and celebrate? Life is our vehicle in which we ride and learn. I challenge all of us to love people and life more. Dance, play, and laugh.

My life and relationships are far from perfect; I am constantly looking for ways to grow and tap into my own potential.

On the last page of Nando' Parrados book, he wrote:

> As we used to say in the mountains, "Breathe. Breathe again. With every breath, you are alive." After all these years, this is still the best advice I can give you: Savor your existence. Live every moment. Do not waste a breath (2006, 284).

What will they say?

References

Blue, G. 2011. LoadSpring Solutions: Work hard, then take a vacation on the company's dime. *Inc.*, May 23. http://www.inc.com/winning-workplaces/201105/loadspring–solutions.html.

Burnison, G. 2010. Listen, learn—and then lead. *Bloomberg Businessweek*, October 1. http://www.businessweek.com/managing/content/sep2010/ca20100928_915118.htm.

Freiberg, K. L., and J. Freiberg. 1996. *Nuts! Southwest airlines' crazy recipe for business and personal success.* New York: Broadway Books.

Isaacson, Walter. 2011. *Steve Jobs.* New York: Simon & Schuster.

Laneri, Raquel. 2009. Body language decoded. *Forbes.com.* http://www.forbes.com/2009/06/23/body-language-first-impression-forbes-woman-leadership-communication.html.

Lybio.net. Wintley Phipps—Amazing Grace. *LYBIO.net.* 11/12/11. http://lybio.net/wintley-phipps-amazing-grace/people.

Martz, S., ed. 1992. *If I had my life to live over.* Kingston, RI: Papier-Mache Press.

O'Daniel, Adam. 2010. Best Places to Work; Work Hard, Play Hard at Goodmortgage.com. *Charlotte Business Journal.* 2010. http://

www.bizjournals.com/charlotte/print-edition/2010/11/05/Work-hard-play-hard-at-Goodmortgage.html.

Parrado, Nando. 2006. *Miracle in the Andes*. New York: Crown Publishing Group.

Robison, J. 2008. How the Ritz-Carlton manages the mystique. *GALLUP Management Journal*, December 11. http://gmj.gallup.com/content/112906/How-RitzCarlton-Manages-Mystique.aspx.

Sharp, I. 2010. *Four seasons: The story of a business philosophy*. Penguin Group.

Tolle, E. 1997. *The power of now: A guide to spiritual enlightenment*. Namaste Publishing.

Vindum, T. 2011. Reduce stress in the great outdoors. *Athleta Chi*, February 23. http://www.athleta.net/chi/2011/02/23/reduce-stress-in-the-great-outdoors/.

Final Funeral Thoughts

1. Find the courage to speak at funerals; people want and need to hear your stories!

2. Plan for your final arrangements; it is a gift you can give to your loved ones.

3. If you decide to leave a gravestone, leave something of yourself behind on it to inspire the living. For instance, Barb Hollister's stone urges her friends and family: "Be Awesome!"

> "It is better to go to a house of mourning than to go to a house of feasting, for death is the destiny of everyone; the living should take this to heart."
> ECCLESIASTES 7:2

CPSIA information can be obtained at www.ICGtesting.com
Printed in the USA
BVOW08*1358110813

328063BV00001B/15/P

9 781604 946611